PLAY LIKE A GIRL

BASKETBALL

BY

EMILIE DUFRESNE

KidHaven
PUBLISHING

Published in 2020 by
KidHaven Publishing, an Imprint of Greenhaven Publishing, LLC
353 3rd Avenue
Suite 255
New York, NY 10010

© 2020 Booklife Publishing

Edited by: Madeline Tyler
Designed by: Danielle Jones

Cataloging-in-Publication Data

Names: Dufresne, Emilie.
Title: Basketball / Emilie Dufresne.
Description: New York : KidHaven Publishing, 2020. | Series: Play
like a girl | Includes glossary and index.
Identifiers: ISBN 9781534530980 (pbk.) | ISBN 9781534530072
(library bound) | ISBN 9781534531307 (6 pack) | ISBN
9781534530928 (ebook)
Subjects: LCSH: Basketball--Juvenile literature.
Classification: LCC GV885.1 D847 2020 | DDC 796.323--dc23

Printed in the United States of America

CPSIA compliance information: Batch #BS19KL: For further information contact Greenhaven
Publishing LLC, New York, New York at 1-844-317-7404.

Please visit our website, www.greenhavenpublishing.com.
For a free color catalog of all our high-quality books, call toll free
1-844-317-7404 or fax 1-844-317-7405.

IMAGE CREDITS

Cover – Andrey_Popov, supparsorn, NPavelN, Photo Melon, margostock, alarich, BigMouse, MyImages – Micha. 3 – Asia Images Group. 4 – Cherdchai charasri, Monkey Business Images, Boris Ryaposov. 5 – Aspen Photo , Monkey Business Images. 6 – Snap2Art, KeremGogus. 7 – A.RICARDO, Gotoenter at English Wikipedia [CC BY 3.0 (https://creativecommons.org/licenses/by/3.0)], via Wikimedia Commons. 8&9 – Tom Wang, LightField Studios, Igor Kovalchuk, hystovskaya katsiaryna, Zilu8, Syda Productions, stockyimages, Vagengeim. 10 – Aspen Photo, Jacob Lund. 11 – Aspen Photo. 12 – ostill, Debby Wong. 13 – Lunatictm. 14 – Boris Ryaposov, ostill. 15 – dnaveh, Monkey Business Images. 16 – PhilipYb Studio. 17 – Sandra Matic, Debby Wong, Bonita R. Cheshier. 18–19 – enterlinedesign. 20 – Hurst Photo, Monkey Business Images. 21 – Aspen Photo, A_Lesik. 22 – ESB Professional, A_Lesik. 23 – Pukhov K, A.RICARDO. 24 – Keeton Gale, By Sergeev Pavel [CCO], from Wikimedia Commons. 25 – By Ultraslansi [CC BY-SA 3.0 (https://creativecommons.org/licenses/by-sa/3.0)], from Wikimedia Commons, By SusanLesch [CC BY 4.0 (https://creativecommons.org/licenses/by/4.0)], from Wikimedia Commons. 26 – Mascha Tace, Mega Pixel, thepiwko. 27 – STILLFX. 28 – The most points scored in a Women's National Basketball Association game is 127 by the Phoenix Mercury (USA) in a 127-124 victory over the Minnesota Lynx (USA) on 24 July 2010, tomertu, Donald Barnat [CC BY-SA 3.0 (https://creativecommons.org/licenses/by-sa/3.0) or GFDL (http://www.gnu.org/copyleft/fdl.html)], via Wikimedia Commons, EVZ. 29 – Australian Paralympic Committee [CC BY-SA 3.0 (https://creativecommons.org/licenses/by-sa/3.0)], via Wikimedia Commons, By UnknownUnknown author [Public domain], via Wikimedia Commons, MyImages – Micha, By Danny Karwoski (Danny Karwoski Facebook) [CC BY-SA 3.0 (https://creativecommons.org/licenses/by-sa/3.0)], via Wikimedia Commons. 30 – Monkey Business Images, Sergey Novikov. Illustrations by Danielle Jones. Images are courtesy of Shutterstock.com. With thanks to Getty Images, Thinkstock Photo and iStockphoto.

CONTENTS

PAGE 4

The Basics

PAGE 6

The Types

PAGE 8

The Lingo

PAGE 10

The Players

PAGE 14

The Uniform

PAGE 16

The Equipment

PAGE 18

The Court

PAGE 20

The Rules

PAGE 22

The Events

PAGE 24

The Ones to Watch

PAGE 26

The Hall of Fame

PAGE 28

The Facts and Stats

PAGE 30

Your Team

PAGE 31

Glossary

PAGE 32

Index

Words that look like <u>this</u> are basketball lingo. Learn more about them on page 8.

Words that look like THIS are explained in the glossary on page 31.

THE BASICS

TEAM HUDDLE

So, you want to play basketball? This book will teach you all about what to say, what to wear, and how to play. From learning the lingo to earning a place in the Hall of Fame, this book will give you the know-how!

GRAB YOUR FRIENDS AND JERSEY – IT'S TIME TO PLAY!

Basketball is a game played by two teams. Each team can have five players on the court at any one time. The players bounce and throw the basketball along the court and try to score points by putting the ball through the OPPOSING team's basket.

Basketball is a very fast-paced game that involves a lot of skill and fitness. There aren't many players on a basketball team compared to other team sports, so they have to run all over the court. They have to be able to work as a team and practice passing, shooting, and <u>dribbling</u> skills to be able to win a game.

Basketball is a **CONTACT SPORT**. However, there are rules restricting how much contact players can make. The official has to decide when too much force has been used or too much contact has been made. If this happens, the official calls a foul and a <u>free throw</u> is given to the team the foul was committed against.

THE TYPES

NETBALL

Netball used to be called women's basketball. This is because basketball was considered a male sport, and netball was seen as the female version. Now, men and women can play both basketball and netball.

NETBALL HAS SEVEN PLAYERS ON EACH TEAM AND PLAYERS SCORE POINTS BY PUTTING THE BALL THROUGH THE OPPONENTS' NET.

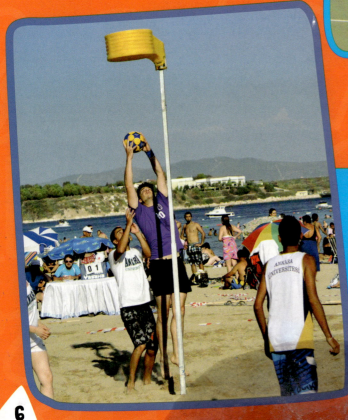

KORFBALL

Korfball is a Dutch sport that is similar to both netball and basketball. Two teams of eight players play against each other with the aim of scoring baskets. The game is unisex, which means both men and women play at the same time.

WHEELCHAIR BASKETBALL

Wheelchair basketball is a VARIATION of basketball for people with physical disabilities. Players use a wheelchair to move across the court, but other than that, the rules are very similar. The court is the same size and the basket is at the same height.

WOMEN'S WHEELCHAIR BASKETBALL WAS FIRST PLAYED AT THE PARALYMPIC GAMES IN 1968.

SLAMBALL

Slamball is very similar to basketball, except that there are four trampolines underneath each basket on the court. This allows players to jump very high into the air to score slam dunks and make trick shots.

LIKE BASKETBALL, SLAMBALL IS ALSO A CONTACT SPORT.

THE LINGO

The lingo, the slang, the vocab. Whatever you call it, learning the words behind specific sports can be a very daunting task! Here are some of the strangest and weirdest words that will help you talk the basketball talk in no time.

TRICK SHOTS

Risky and incredible shots that are unlikely to score but are very impressive to watch.

TRAVEL

To walk or run while holding the ball instead of dribbling it. This is an **ILLEGAL** move.

FREE THROW

Throws given to a team when a foul has been committed against them. Baskets scored this way are only worth one point.

OPEN

When a player is not being guarded by a member of the opposite team and they will easily be able to catch the ball.

DRIBBLING

Bouncing the ball as you walk or run with it.

JUMP BALL

Used at the beginning of the match or to restart play. Two opposing players face each other, the ball is thrown high into the air by an official, and both players jump to try to get possession of the ball.

GUARD

When players closely watch and stand near players of the opposing team to make sure that they don't gain possession of the ball.

SLAM DUNKS

Basketball shots where a player jumps very high into the air and pushes the ball downward through the hoop.

THREE-POINT LINE

Any shot scored from behind the line is worth three points and is called a 3-pointer; any shot from within the line is only worth two points.

SCREENS

When a player stands in front of a member of the opposing team to stop them from defending the ball and provide an open route for other players to travel.

REBOUNDS

When one player shoots and misses the basket, and another player catches the ball to continue playing.

LAYUPS

Two-part shots that are made by jumping into the air and using one hand to bounce the ball off of the backboard so that it falls into the net.

POSSESSION

When a member of your team has the ball.

THE PLAYERS

Each team is allowed five players on the court at any one time during a basketball game. Each of these players has two different roles: an offensive role and a defensive role. Players must be able to quickly switch between these two roles.

1. POINT GUARD

Offensive: The point guard is the player responsible for driving the offense. They need to get the ball to the opponents' side of the court and help to put any plans in play so that their team can score points. They should be good scorers from the three-point line.

Defensive: When defending, point guards stay near the three-point line at their end of the court and try not to let the point guard on the opposing team pass into the shooting area.

2. SHOOTING GUARD

Offensive: As the name suggests, the shooting guard is the main shooter on the team. It is their job to make sure they are <u>open</u> and ready to shoot. They should be good at scoring in many different ways, including 3-pointers and <u>layups</u>.

Defensive: Shooting guards need to stop their opponents from getting past them and take back <u>possession</u> of the ball.

3. SMALL FORWARD

Offensive: This player needs to be very **VERSATILE** and be able to slip into other roles if needed. They are there to score and to help the center and power forwards with <u>rebounds</u>.

Defensive: The small forwards should be able to <u>mark</u> multiple players at once and stop their opponents from creating scoring opportunities.

4. POWER FORWARD

Offensive: These players are expected to play and shoot from the corners, wings, and under the basket. They should gain possession of rebounds and create <u>screens</u>.

Defensive: Power forwards defend the net, corners, and wings. It's their job to make it hard for the opposition to pass into the shooting area and score any close-range shots.

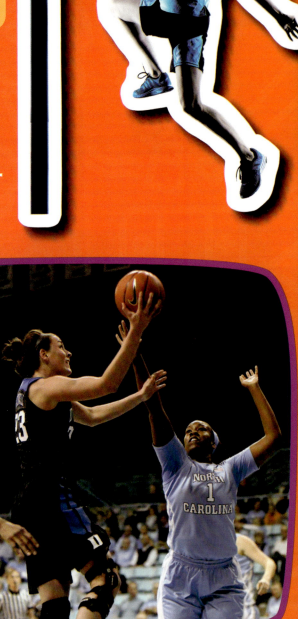

5. CENTER

Offensive: The center will spend most of their time under the basket. They make screens to protect other players and make sure the right player has the ball at the right time.

Defensive: The center has to try to block any shots from the opponents and gain possession of rebounds whenever possible. If successful, they then have to quickly change to offensive play and get the ball to the opponents' side of the court.

THIS IS ONE WAY THAT PLAYERS CAN PLACE THEMSELVES ON THE COURT.

THE UNIFORM

Basketball is a fast-paced sport that is a very good form of exercise. It works both your CARDIOVASCULAR SYSTEM and your muscles. Players are constantly jumping, shooting, and running up and down the court.

It is important to make sure you have the right gear so that you can play your best. A basketball player's clothing usually consists of a baggy sleeveless top or jersey. On the bottom, players wear baggy shorts that nearly hit the knee.

JERSEY

JERSEY

BAGGY SHORTS

BAGGY SHORTS

BASKETBALL SHOES

Basketball players also need to wear shoes that are specially **ADAPTED** for the sport. Basketball shoes are very good at **ABSORBING** shock from jumping and running. They also have very good grip so that you don't slip or slide when you need to change direction quickly while running.

Often these shoes come quite high up your ankles. These are called high-tops. Basketball shoes are often made like this to protect your ankles. They can help prevent twists and sprains.

NOW THAT YOU HAVE YOUR UNIFORM, IT'S TIME TO GET THE EQUIPMENT.

THE EQUIPMENT

THE BALL

Basketballs are a standardized object. For women, the ball **CIRCUMFERENCE** must be no larger than 28.5 inches (72.4 cm).

28.5 IN

Standardized objects make sure that the game is fair by making sure every game is played with the same type of equipment every time.

THE HOOP

The hoop must have a diameter of 18 inches (46 cm). The hoop's rim is 10 feet (3 m) above the ground.

THE BACKBOARD

Luckily, to help you score points, there is a backboard attached to the hoop. The board is 72 inches (183 cm) wide and 42 inches (107 cm) tall. The inner rectangle on the board is 24 inches (61 cm) wide and 18 inches (46 cm) tall.

Players can bounce the ball off the backboard at different angles. This makes it easier to score points. Very skilled players can score without using the backboard or hitting the hoop with the ball. This type of shot is called "nothing but net."

THE COURT

Baseline 50 feet

BASELINE
The line that shows when the ball has gone out of play at either end of the court.

THREE-POINT LINE
If a player scores from this line or farther away from the hoop, then they score three points instead of two.

BASKET

FREE THROW LINE
Where free throws can be taken from.

CENTER CIRCLE
Where the jump ball happens.

SIDELINE

The line that shows when the ball has gone out of play at the sides of the court.

BACKBOARD

HALF-COURT LINE

The line that marks the middle of the court and lets players know which half they are in. When a team playing offensively takes the ball past this line and into their opponents' side of the court, they cannot take the ball back past this line.

THE RULES

Depending on whether you are playing at college level, for the Women's National Basketball Association (WNBA), or internationally, the rules of basketball can be different. Here we will focus on the WNBA rules.

TIMING

The game is split into four 10-minute quarters. Between the second and third there is a 15-minute break for halftime.

In international and college games, each quarter is also 10 minutes long.

RULES FOR ALL PLAYERS

- Players cannot foul other players by purposefully using physical contact to make them lose control of the ball

- Players cannot kick the ball or hit the ball with their fist

- Defenders cannot touch the ball as it is traveling down toward the net

RULES FOR THE OFFENSE

IF YOUR TEAM HAS THE BALL, YOU ARE PLAYING OFFENSE.

- Players cannot <u>travel</u> with the ball

- A player cannot dribble, stop and hold the ball, and then start dribbling again

- If the offensive team puts the ball out of bounds, the defending team gets control of the ball

- Once the offense passes the half-court line, they cannot travel backwards into their half of the court unless the defense knocks it back into their half

- When a team wins back possession in their half, they only have **10** seconds to get the ball out of their half of the court, otherwise a foul is given against their team

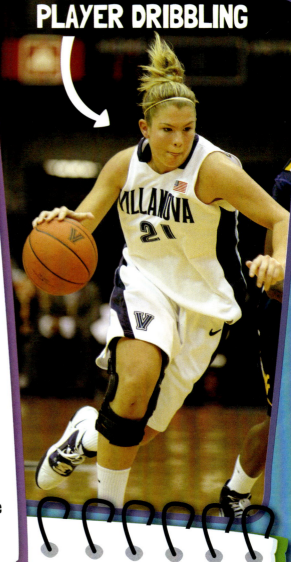

PLAYER DRIBBLING

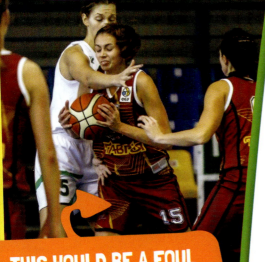

THIS WOULD BE A FOUL BECAUSE THIS PLAYER IS HOLDING THE OTHER PLAYER BACK.

RULES FOR THE DEFENSE

IF THE OPPOSING TEAM HAS THE BALL, YOU ARE PLAYING DEFENSE. THE MAIN RULE FOR THE DEFENSE IS NOT TO FOUL. IF THE DEFENSE FOULS, IT MEANS THEIR OPPONENTS COULD GET A FREE THROW.

Examples of fouls committed against other players:

- Hitting
- Slapping
- Pushing
- Holding

THE EVENTS

RECREATIONAL AND REGIONAL TEAMS

If you have a school team, or a team that plays RECREATIONALLY, and you want to start competing, there are lots of ways you can get involved. Ask a teacher, parent, or sports coach how to join a local league.

THE BIG LEAGUES

As basketball players get better and better, they can start playing at higher levels. After regional games come national ones. This means you play teams from all over your country. Then comes playing internationally, which means playing for your country. There are lots of tournaments for different CONTINENTS around the world, including Africa, Asia, Europe, and the Americas.

AMATEUR BASKETBALL TEAM PRACTICING

UKRAINE NATIONAL TEAM, 2016

WORLD TOURNAMENTS

International competitions are competitions in which countries compete from all over the world. There are lots of different events for basketball in which players from countries all over the world play. Some of these include the **FIBA** Basketball World Cup, the **IWBF** International Wheelchair World Championships, and the **COMMONWEALTH** Games.

THE OLYMPICS

One of the most **PRESTIGIOUS** world tournaments is the Olympics. Lots of countries compete in a variety of games, one of which is basketball. Women's basketball is a sport in both the Summer Olympics and Paralympic Games. The United States has the most successful Olympic women's basketball team. They have won gold eight times and even won six times in a row from 1996–2016.

BRAZIL VS. FRANCE AT THE 2016 RIO OLYMPIC GAMES

THE ONES TO WATCH

There are some very talented female basketball players to look out for. Let's find out some more about them.

SANDRINE GRUDA

FACT FILE:

Date of Birth:	June 25, 1987
Country of Birth:	France
Height:	6'4" (1.93 m)
Position:	Center

Gruda has played for both the French national team and for the WNBA. She has helped her country win multiple medals in the EuroBasket tournament and took home silver in the 2012 Olympic Games. Her team also won the WNBA championship in 2016.

BREANNA STEWART

FACT FILE:

Date of Birth:	August 27, 1994
Country of Birth:	USA
Height:	6'4" (1.93 m)
Position:	Power Forward/Center

Stewart is considered one of the best basketball players in the world and has already had numerous achievements at a young age. She won gold at her first Olympic Games in 2016 and was awarded Most Valuable Player of the WNBA in 2018.

PLAY LIKE A GIRL

PLAY LIKE A GIRL

ALBA TORRENS

FACT FILE:

Date of Birth:
August 30, 1989

Country of Birth:
Spain

Height:
6'3" (1.91 m)

Position:
Small Forward

Torrens is considered one of the best European basketball players since 2000. Even when playing for youth teams, it was obvious she had great talent, as she won several gold medals in youth tournaments. In her adult career, she has won two gold medals at European tournaments and silver at the 2016 Olympic Games, among others.

LIZ CAMBAGE

FACT FILE:

Date of Birth:
August 18, 1991

Country of Birth:
UK

Height:
6'8" (2.03 m)

Position:
Center

British-born Australian Liz Cambage already has some impressive records at a young age. She currently holds the WNBA single-game scoring record, with a total of 53 points scored in one game. She has also helped her national team win bronze in the 2012 Olympic Games and gold in the 2018 Commonwealth Games.

THE HALL

There is a great history of female basketball players. Let's take a look at some of the best of the best.

Diana Taurasi is a heavily **DECORATED** basketball player with numerous awards and medals. She is known for scoring in even the stickiest of situations. In 2011, she was named as one of the WNBA's Top 15 Players of All Time. Throughout her career, she has earned multiple honors.

American-Israeli Sue Bird is a powerful point guard. She is considered one of the best players to have ever graced the game of basketball. With three WNBA championship titles and four Olympic gold medals, to name a few of her prestigious achievements, she more than deserves a place in the basketball Hall of Fame.

Lisa Leslie had a long and fruitful career. Winning four Olympic golds in a row with the USA team and being the first person to slam dunk in a WNBA game are only a few of her many achievements. In fact, she has been given nearly 40 different awards throughout her basketball career.

Dawn Staley is not only a great basketball player in her own right, but also an impressive coach. Having won three Olympic golds as a player, Staley has gone on to help coach the USA's international women's team to win three Olympic golds.

THE FACTS AND STATS

THE USA HAS WON THE MOST OLYMPIC GOLD MEDALS IN WOMEN'S BASKETBALL, WITH 8 OVERALL.

MAŁGORZATA DYDEK IS THE TALLEST WOMAN IN THE HISTORY OF BASKETBALL. MEASURING IN AT 7'2" (2.18 M) TALL, SHE OFTEN TOWERED OVER OTHER PLAYERS.

HOME 124   07:29   GUEST 127
PERIOD 4
BONUS   POSS   BONUS
FOULS   SHOT CLOCK   FOULS
30   :17   32

THE RECORD FOR THE MOST POINTS SCORED IN A WNBA GAME IS HELD BY THE PHOENIX MERCURY TEAM, WHICH SCORED AN IMPRESSIVE 127 POINTS TO TAKE THE VICTORY OVER THE MINNESOTA LYNX IN 2010.

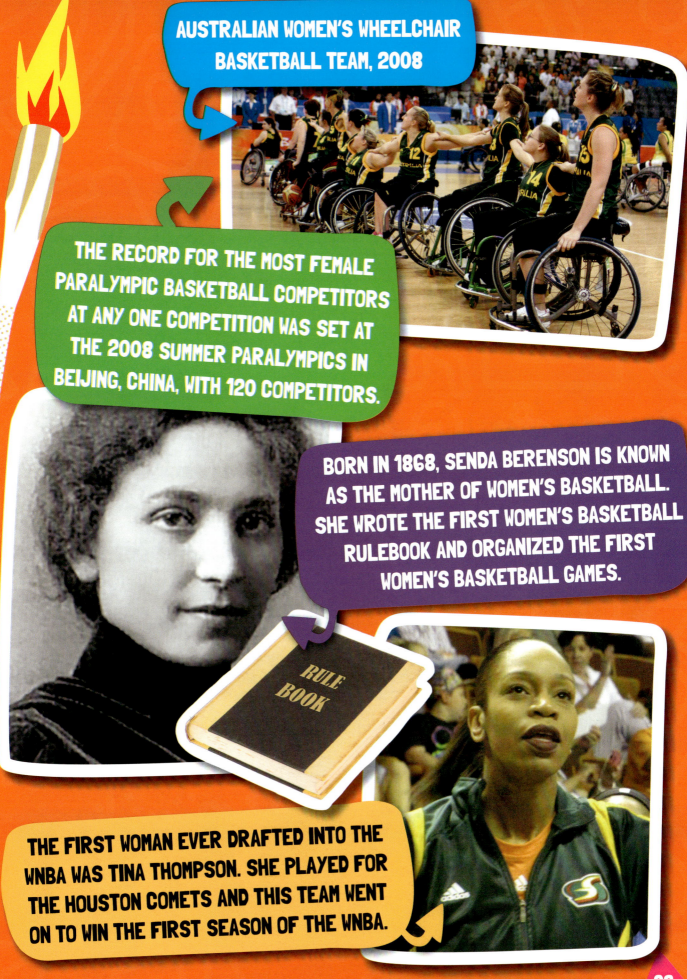

AUSTRALIAN WOMEN'S WHEELCHAIR BASKETBALL TEAM, 2008

THE RECORD FOR THE MOST FEMALE PARALYMPIC BASKETBALL COMPETITORS AT ANY ONE COMPETITION WAS SET AT THE 2008 SUMMER PARALYMPICS IN BEIJING, CHINA, WITH 120 COMPETITORS.

BORN IN 1868, SENDA BERENSON IS KNOWN AS THE MOTHER OF WOMEN'S BASKETBALL. SHE WROTE THE FIRST WOMEN'S BASKETBALL RULEBOOK AND ORGANIZED THE FIRST WOMEN'S BASKETBALL GAMES.

RULE BOOK

THE FIRST WOMAN EVER DRAFTED INTO THE WNBA WAS TINA THOMPSON. SHE PLAYED FOR THE HOUSTON COMETS AND THIS TEAM WENT ON TO WIN THE FIRST SEASON OF THE WNBA.

YOUR TEAM

If basketball sounds like the sport for you, why not try to get a team together? Ask all your friends if they want to give it a go. If you have a gym or an outdoor court in your school or where you live, why not try it?

Basketball is fun to play with friends. It can help you stay fit and healthy, too.

YOUR NAME HERE

YOU NEVER KNOW, YOU MIGHT BE IN THE HALL OF FAME ONE DAY!

GLOSSARY

absorbing   taking in or soaking up

adapted   to be changed for a specific use

amateur   someone who does something for fun rather than professionally

cardiovascular system   a system in the body that circulates blood around the body

circumference   the distance all the way around a circular object

Commonwealth   a group of countries, including the UK, Canada, and Australia, that used to be part of the British Empire

contact sport   a sport in which players' bodies are allowed to come into contact

continents   very large areas of land that are often made up of many countries, such as Africa and Europe

decorated   in a profession, this is when you have been given awards, medals, or trophies for your work

FIBA   Fédération Internationale de Basketball; an organization that governs the international game of basketball

illegal   an action that is not allowed within the rules of a sport

IWBF   International Wheelchair Basketball Federation; an organization that governs the worldwide sport of wheelchair basketball

opposing   on the team playing against you

prestigious   having an important and highly regarded status

recreationally   to do something for fun rather than professionally

variation   a changed or slightly different version of something

versatile   able to be adapted in order to fit many different functions or activities

WNBA   Women's National Basketball Association; a women's professional basketball league in the United States

INDEX

B

backboards 9, 17, 19

C

court 4–5, 7, 10, 12–14, 18–19, 21, 30

D

defense 9–12, 20–21

dribbling 5, 8, 21

F

fouls 5, 8, 21

H

hoops 9, 16–18

J

jumps 7–9, 14–15, 18

M

medals 24–26, 28

O

offense 10–12, 19, 21

Olympics 23–28

opposition 4, 8–10, 12, 21

P

Paralympics 7, 23, 29

positions 10–13, 24–25

possession 8–9, 12

R

rebounds 11–12

S

shooting 5, 7–12, 14, 17

T

throws 4–5, 8, 18, 21

tournaments 22–25

traveling 8–9, 20–21